INTRODUCTION TO THE SCIENCE OF EDUCATION

INTRODUCTION TO THE SCIENCE OF EDUCATION

INTRODUCTION TO THE SCIENCE OF EDUCATION

BINOY KUMAR SARKAR

Translator
MAJOR B. D. BASU

GYAN

Published by

GYAN

Gyan Publishing House
5, Ansari Road
Daryaganj, New Delhi-110002
Phone: 011-47034999, 9811692060
E-mail: books@gyanbooks.com

Distribution Network
gyanbooks.com
India, USA, Canada, UK, Australia

ISBN: 978-93-7169-291-5 (PB)

First Published, 1913

2nd Impression 2025

Printed at: Gyan Press, Delhi.

INTRODUCTION TO THE SCIENCE OF EDUCATION
Author: BINOY KUMAR SARKAR

INTRODUCTION

TO THE

SCIENCE OF EDUCATION

BY

BENOY KUMAR SARKAR, M.A.

Professor of Political Science, National Council of Education, Bengal

TRANSLATED FROM THE BENGALI

BY

MAJOR B. D. BASU, I.M.S. (Retired)

Editor of "The Sacred Books of the Hindus"
Author of "Indian Medicinal Plants"

LONGMANS, GREEN, AND CO.

39 PATERNOSTER ROW, LONDON

NEW YORK, BOMBAY AND CALCUTTA

1913

TRANSLATOR'S PREFACE

THE Bengali work entitled *Introduction to the Science of Education*, by Professor Benoy Kumar Sarkar, M.A., of the National Council of Education, Bengal, was published at Calcutta in August, 1910. The expectations that were raised by this Introduction have since been fulfilled to a great extent by the publication of the author's *National Education in Ancient Greece*, *The Study of Language*, *Lessons on English* in three parts, and *Lessons on Sanskrit* in four parts. *Lessons* on Botany, Chemistry, and Mathematics according to the Professor's Inductive Method of Teaching are in preparation and will be soon out in Bengali.

The present work is a free translation of Professor Sarkar's own Introduction to this Educational Series, and has been undertaken at the suggestion of several of our distinguished educationists and men of letters. The author's *début* as well as the volumes that followed it were welcomed by the men of light and leading in the community as well as all sections of the Press, both vernacular and English, as the products of a highly original and scientific intellect and as indications of the new spirit of bold and independent enterprise in the realms of thought and fields of scholarship for which there are few opportunities in India.

In the Preface to Professor Sarkar's linguistic volumes Principal Brajendra Nath Seal, M.A., Ph.D., recorded his opinion that "there can be no doubt that it will be found to be a healthy and stimulating force in the Indian educational world of to-day" and that "his scheme of educational works is based on sound and advanced ideas of educational science, and as such, is well calculated to impart a valuable stimulus to the diffusion of culture in the country." Regarding the same Mr. P. N. Bose, B.Sc. (London), F.G.S., M.R.A.S., has remarked that it is "on such an elaborate plan and embraces such a wide variety of subjects which would be interesting and instructive, not only to all educated Indians, but probably to cultured men of other nationalities, that I almost regret it should be written in a provincial vernacular."

The lines of educational reform suggested and initiated in the volumes published up to date are not due to any hasty and impatient discontent with the existing state of things, but are due to the matured convictions of a well-read and versatile scholar, a systematic thinker, and a practical worker in the field of education. Professor Sarkar is one of the most distinguished alumni of the Calcutta University. He has had a very brilliant academic career, having topped the list of successful candidates in both the Matriculation and Graduation Examinations of his year. He was first in the First Division in both the Honours subjects, History and English, offered by him at the B.A. Examination, and was elected to the Government of India State Scholarship for the prosecution of studies in Oxford or Cambridge University.

Professor Sarkar's theories have grown out

of the needs of actual work as a teacher and an organizer of educational institutions, and are the outcome of his practical experiences in several capacities. He has supplemented his scholastic education with extensive tours in India, and has associated himself intimately with the literary and educational movements of the country. His scheme for fostering and "protecting" vernacular literature by a system of endowments supporting men of letters and enabling a complete devotion to the growth of literature with the object of making it the medium of instruction in all subjects and in all stages of educational life, has been warmly appreciated in all quarters; and already the scheme is being acted on in some provinces. The aim and end of his efforts in this connection have been, in his own words, that "in the course of ten years we can have the best literary treasures of the world in our own literature, that we can have the thoughts and investigations of Plato, Herbert Spencer, Guizot, Hegel, and other European philosophers, through the medium of our own language, and that in no time the education of these provinces can grow into one that is *natural* and really national." Himself a good Sanskrit scholar, he is deeply interested in the propagation of Hindu Literature both in India and abroad—and this wholly in the non-sectarian and non-political spirit, to further the cause of Comparative Literature, Science, and Sociology. He looks forward to the days when the facts and phenomena of Indian life and culture will not be passed over by the savants of the West and Doctors of European and American Universities as merely "oriental," "non-economic," "non-political," or even "pre-political" and "pre-economic," but will be dispassionately studied as reflecting new types of social conditions which can be neglected only by inflicting serious loss on the Human Sciences.

His work in the actual field of education has also been a varied one. As a Professor of the Bengal National College, Calcutta, managed as the independent metropolitan institution under the National Council of Education, Bengal, by men like Dr. Rashbehari Ghose, M.A., D.L., C.S.I., C.I.E., and Sir Gooroodas

Banerjee, Kt., M.A., D.L., Ph.D., late Vice-Chancellor, Calcutta University, he has earned the reputation of a devoted and strenuous worker. The following remarks are taken from the Council's Calendar for 1906–7, drawn up by Mr. (now Honourable Justice) A. Chaudhuri, M.A. (Cal.), B.A. (Cantab.), and Babu Hirendranath Datta, M.A., B.L.: "He takes special pleasure in teaching boys of the lower forms, and his suggestions for improvement in methods of teaching are always helpful." The following, again, is taken from the Report for 1908: "During the last two years he had been carrying on experiments both in and out of school so as to ascertain the best method to be pursued in teaching the various subjects at the several stages of development. He has already reduced into form his thoughts on the teaching of Bengali, Sanskrit, English, Arithmetic, Botany, Zoology, Chemistry, and the Historical subjects."

His success as a teacher has been evidenced by the popularity of his Lecture-notes on Economics, European History, and Political Science. His analytical method combines lucidity with depth and brings home to the pupils the salient points they ought to know, and is in fact altogether a new thing in the Indian tutorial world. These lectures, together with the private lessons to his brothers and pupils at home, have been published under the name of the *Aids to General Culture.* The series consists of compilations on (1) History of Ancient Europe, (2) History of Mediæval Europe, (3) Constitutions of Modern States, (4) Economics, (5) Political Science, and (6) History of English Literature, and suits the B.A. Honours and partially the M.A. Degree requirements of Indian Universities. According to competent authorities the works "show wide knowledge of the subject matter and are evidently the outcome of a mind trained in habits of clear, patient, and accurate thinking." And while indicative of the comprehensive and encyclopædic conception that finds its full display in the educational series in Bengali, the history of the composition of the General Culture Series brings out an important characteristic of the Professor's educational life. For the series is incidentally a protest against the narrow and one-sided development that the Indian Universities promote. Says he in the Preface : "It has had its origin in my practice, during the last three or four years, of leading my brothers and pupils at home through these subjects, *irrespective of school-work.* It seeks to present in a handy form the more important and generally accepted ideas of recognized authorities on those branches of study without which no education may be called liberal."

It may be mentioned that some of his scholars who did not receive any help from the Indian Universities have been acquitting themselves very creditably in the Harvard, Yale, Michigan, and Wisconsin Universities of America.

Besides being a Professor and Member of the National Council of Education, he is the founder and director of several educational institutions in Bengal, where his pedagogic theories are carried into practice as far as possible under the conditions of life obtaining throughout the province. The following is the Professor's "Educational Creed" which gives the shortest account of his pedagogic system :

A. *General.*

I. Aim and Criterion of Education twofold : the man must be (i) intellectually, a discoverer of truths and a pioneer of learning ; (ii) morally, an organizer of institutions and a leader of men.

II. Moral Training to be imparted not through lessons culled from moral and religious textbooks, but through arrangements by which the student is actually made to develop habits of self-sacrifice and devotion to the interests of others by undertaking works of philanthropy and social service.

III. To build up character and determine the aim or mission of life, (i) the "design," plan, and personal responsibility of a single guide-philosopher-friend, and (ii) the control of the whole life and career of the student, are indispensable. These circumstances provide the pre-condition for true Spiritual Education.

IV. Educational Institutions and Movements must not be made planks in political, industrial, social, or religious agitations and propagandas, but controlled and governed by the Science of Education based on the rational grounds of Sociology.

B. *Tutorial.*

I. Even the most elementary course must have a Multiplicity of subjects with due inter-relation and co-ordination. Up to a certain stage the training must be encyclopædic and as comprehensive as possible.

II. The mother-tongue must be the Medium of instruction in all subjects and through all standards. And if in India the provincial languages are really inadequate and poor, the educationists must make it a point to develop and enrich them within the shortest possible time by a system of patronage and endowments on the "protective principle."

III. The *sentence*, not word, must be the basis of Language-training, whether in Inflexional or Analytical tongues—even in Sanskrit; and the Inductive Method of proceeding from the known to the unknown, concrete to the abstract, facts and phenomena to general principles, is to be the tutorial method in all branches of learning.

IV. Two Foreign languages besides English and at least two provincial vernaculars must be made compulsory for all Higher Culture in India.

C. *Organizational.*

I. Examinations must be daily. The day's work must be finished and tested during the day. And terms of academic life as well as the system of giving credit should be not by years or months but according to subjects or portions of subjects studied. Steady and constant discipline, both intellectual and moral, are possible only under these conditions.

II. The Laboratory and Environment of student-life must be the whole world of men and things. The day's routine must therefore provide opportunities for self-sacrifice, devotion, recreations, excursions, etc., as well as pure intellectual work. There should consequently be no long holidays or periodical vacations except when necessitated by pedagogic interests.

Among the persons working or being trained up under this system some are those scholars who have been showing excellent results in the foreign Universities mentioned above, and others have displayed their ability in the fields of Historical Research, Literary Criticism, Sanskrit Literature, and Indian Antiquities.

The most important of Professor Sarkar's contributions to educational thought and literature are his *Lessons on Sanskrit without Grammar*. Mahamahopadhyaya Pandit Adityaram Bhattacharyya, M.A., late Professor of Sanskrit Literature, Muir College, and Fellow, Allahabad University, writes about these books: "I write this in my appreciation of your effort to facilitate and popularize the study of Sanskrit. Your method to teach Sanskrit without the learner's going through a first course of grammar merits trial. At the very outset the attempt looks somewhat revolutionary. But in other fields it is such revolutionary departures from the old track that has hastened the advance of arts and sciences."

RAIBAHDUR[1] Mr. Srish Chandra Basu, B.A.,

---

[1] Translator (and annotator) of Bhattaji Dikshita's *Siddhanta Kaumudi*, the *Upani-*

of the Provincial Civil Service, author of the *Ashtadhyayi* of *Panini* (M.A. Textbook, London University), gives the following account of the method adopted in these volumes:

"The scheme of Sanskrit works in Professor Benoy Kumar Sarkar's pedagogic series is based on the conception that any language, whether inflectional or analytical, living or dead, can be learnt exactly in the method in which the mother-tongue is acquired. No preliminary training in the generalizations and definitions of grammar is therefore required, and the student may be at once introduced to the *sentence* as the unit of thought and expression.

"By a skilful and systematic application of this method, Professor Sarkar has been able to build up, through lessons and exercises in translation, conversation, questions and answers, and correction of errors, a textbook in Sanskrit which serves the *double purpose*

---

shads, *Vedanta Sutras*, and the *Mitakshara* in the "Sacred Books of the Hindus Series."

of a guide to composition and a series of primers on Sanskrit literature. From this series of books the reader can master not only the necessary rules of Sanskrit Grammar, but also will be familiar with some of the most important passages of standard classics, e.g., *Raghu-vansam*, *Kumâr-sambhavam*, *Râmâyanam*, and *Manu Sanhitâ*, adaptations or originals of which the author has incorporated in his book as specimens of narrative, historical, poetical, and other styles.

"In applying to the study of Sanskrit principles and methods that have been utilized in modern languages in Europe, Professor Sarkar has demonstrated, through practical illustrations, *lesson by lesson*, that the most highly inflectional languages may, with considerable economy of time and labour and other pedagogic advantages, be reduced to the same method of teaching and treatment as those languages which are not bound hard and fast by Grammar. To all students of Sanskrit language and literature Professor Sarkar's series cannot but be eminently useful and instructive; and scholars interested in the art of teaching and the history of Sanskrit learning cannot but note the considerable improvement on the existing Readers and Primers that are in most cases mere imitations or occasional modifications of the really original works of Pandit Ishwar Chandra Vidyasagara, C.I.E., whose genius succeeded in simplifying and adapting Panini for the use of students in Bengal.

"The method of the pioneer of Sanskrit learning can no longer be profitably used under the altered conditions of the times; and it is desirable that the new method should have a fair trial in our secondary schools in the interest of educational reform."

Rai Sarat Chandra Das Bahadur, C.I.E., the great Tibetan traveller and Oriental scholar, in the paper submitted to the Conference of Orientalists held at Simla under the presidency of the Educational Member of the Government of India in 1911, recommends the works in the following words:

"If Sanskrit for ordinary purposes could be learnt without grammar it would undoubtedly be a great gain. I am of opinion that this is quite possible. Professor Benoy Kumar Sarkar, M.A., of the National College, Calcutta, has shown the method in his excellent manuals which are now being printed in Calcutta. No preliminary training in the generalizations and definitions of grammar is required. I suggest that a fair trial be given to his method in the tols and schools of this country, for in my opinion it will encourage the study of Sanskrit."

Professor Sarkar is also the author of works that are of historical, literary, and sociological importance. He has contributed to the "Sacred Books of the Hindus Series" published by the Panini office, Allahabad, an annotated English edition of the Sanskrit work *Sukraniti*, or Sukrâchâryya's System of Morals (Social, Economic, and Political), and is collecting materials for a work in English on the Economic and Political Theories of the Hindus on the same lines as the History of *Political Theories* by Professor Dunning of the Columbia University, U.S.A. He has rendered into Bengali *Raj-Tarangini*, or the Annals of Kashmir in Sanskrit, by the poet-historian Kalhan. A contribution to the study of Hindu Sociology, in English, has been made ready for the press under the title *A Socio-Religious Institution of Bengal.* And in the course of his studies he has been preparing notes for the following works to be first published in English: (1) *Lectures on the Science of History*—an investigation of general principles underlying the course of Universal History; (2) *An Introduction to the History of Indian Civilization*—an attempt to elucidate the working of the forces, both political as well as non-political, and national as well as international, that have shaped the Indian national character—a study and interpretation of available materials from the Biological standpoint; (3) *Studies in Sanskrit Literature*—Literary and Sociological.

Besides the systematic works that have been published and are going through the press or are in preparation, Professor Sarkar has contributed Lectures and Essays on educational and literary subjects, both in English and Bengali, to Monthly Reviews. A small treatise on the *Science of History and the Hope of*

Mankind has been published recently in England by Messrs. Longmans, Green & Co. The following extract from the Preface would give an idea of the work :

"My object was to survey, not historically but according to the philosophico-comparative method, the phenomena of civilization and point out the laws or generalizations that may be deduced out of the facts of universal history.

"Human civilization, like physical facts and phenomena, requires to be studied in such a way as to lead to the detection of uniformities in the sequences and coexistences of social events and movements. History has to be put on the same level with physics and other Natural Sciences; so that predictions may be possible in the social world as in the physical."

In the treatise there is an attempt at explaining the ups and downs of nations by referring to the laws of life. And it contains a somewhat novel interpretation of the facts of European history. The truth that the destiny of a nation is not the making of its own people solely but is moulded by the interaction of World Forces is very ably brought out.

TRANSLATOR'S PREFACE

Three volumes of Essays in Bengali have been published in the course of the year—(1) Historical, (2) Educational, and (3) Miscellaneous. These have been very valuable contributions to Bengali literature as much for the originality and high seriousness of the thought as for the clear and able presentation of the subject matter, and the vigour and eloquence of style. And the distinguished *littérateurs* who have contributed prefaces to his works have remarked on the signal achievements in Bengali language and thought wrought thereby.

The Professor's conception of History as the science of the whole of human affairs, and suggestions as to how the facts and phenomena of Indian history should be interpreted and explained so that the idea of a living, moving, growing, and expanding people may be always before the mind's eye, have been expressed in a language that is clear, simple, and yet powerful. And there is a distinctively Hindu note pervading his historical studies, inasmuch as they bring out "the Vedantic and transcendental conception that History is the record of the progress of the human soul, is the positive register of the truths of morality and religion, and that it is essentially a branch of *Dharma Sâstra.*"

At the last Bengal Literary Conference held at Chinsurah in the first week of March, Professor Sarkar read a very thoughtful and instructive paper on Religious Education, the topic that has been agitating public mind and receiving Government's serious attention for some time past. "In Education as in Industry, Professor Sarkar is an advocate of the *Domestic* as opposed to the *Factory System*, and made out his case for it in a most consistent and scientific way. In the course of his arguments he gave an account of the nature and method of Religious education prevalent in Europe and America, criticized Western pedagogic ideals and philosophy of life, and discussed such problems as the antagonism between culture and faith and the rivalry of religious denominations. His conclusion is that what passes for religious education in the Western Universities is only a part of Historical and Philosophical instruction, and that real spiritual culture cannot be promoted in educational institutions of the type known in Europe and America. He discusses the claims of the Day school, Boarding school, Residential system, and Teaching Universities, and finds that these can never have the atmosphere and environment for the 'education' of the heavenward instincts of the soul. Spiritual Education worth the name can be promoted only under conditions of personal love and responsibility that were supplied in the *Homes of Preceptors* in Ancient India. The Professor gives a graphic and glorious account of the Hindu pedagogic system that has produced through the ages a continuous race of men and women—Pânini, Chandragupta, Vasistha, Maitreyi, Râmprasâd, Râni Bhavâni, Siváji, and Râmkrishna—who may be ranked among the greatest of world's thinkers and actors. He concludes by pointing out the message and mission of modern India to humanity."[1]

[1] Extract from the *Collegian*, an All-India Journal of Education conducted by Professors of Calcutta.

The close logic and philosophic treatment of the subject matter make the paper a masterpiece of Bengali literature. Above all, there are a seriousness and sincerity, a high moral tone and warmth of feeling that characterize all his works.

The Bengali works have received recognition beyond the author's own province. Nearly all of these have been translated into Hindi, the most widely used of all the provincial vernaculars of India, and some of them are passing through the press just now. Translations into other vernaculars also are in progress.

It would have appeared that Professor Sarkar is not merely a man of letters. He is also a man of action who has devoted himself completely to public work. He has been maintaining several "schools of modern culture" in his province, and is an active supporter of institutions and movements for the promotion of original research, industrial experiments, and development of literature. His ability as an organizer is further shown in his creation of a scholarship fund which is now supporting some fifteen students in their studies in some of the first-grade American Universities. His friend and colleague in all this branch of work has been Professor Radhakumud Mookerji, M.A., of the National Council of Education, Bengal, author of the well-known work on *The History of Indian Shipping and Maritime Activity from the Earliest Times*, another young man inspired by the same ideals.

Professor Sarkar is still quite a young man, about to complete his twenty-sixth year. He was a Master of Arts while yet in his teens. The example of so much work achieved by such a young age must be rare in the annals of youth itself. The brilliant promise of his early years will, we hope, have a richer fulfilment in the many years of work and activity that are still before him. He is in all respects a remarkable person, in whom have met all that is noble, all that is great in modern Bengal. In his selfless devotion to the cause of national education and literature, and in the boldness and originality of his thought and action, he is one of the finest products of the non-political national idealism that is now inspiring the more thoughtful section of educated India, and but continues the tradition of the greatest of her sons born within recent times—the philanthropist Iswar Chunder Vidyâsâgar, the educationist Bhudev Mukerjee, and the missionary Swâmi Vivekânanda.

B. D. BASU.

PANINI OFFICE, ALLAHABAD,
June 20, 1912.

CONTENTS

SECTION I

METHODS OF HUMAN SCIENCE

TO acquire perfect mastery over a subject it is necessary to adopt diverse methods of study. And the truths that are discovered with the help of these various methods of investigation have to be placed in a systematic order, their mutual relations and co-ordinations have to be explained and adjusted, and their unity and harmony organized on a rational basis before they can constitute what is technically called a science.

A variety of scientific methods is specially necessary for the investigation of subjects that are very complex in their nature, and phenomena which are intimately connected and inextricably wound up with extraneous and alien matters. For in the cases of matters that bear the influence of diverse agencies the truth which is arrived at by one method of study is not necessarily the same as is disclosed when another method is adopted. All the various methods of truth-investigation must therefore be pursued to get hold of the whole truth; otherwise our knowledge will be partial and one-sided.

Thus, for example, Religious and Political subjects, Social and Legal topics, and phenomena of Art and Literature which are essentially human in their nature, having their origin in the manifold aspects of man and his life, and the arts and institutions of civilization which depend for their progression, retrogression, and evolution upon the living and active faculties of the human mind, present peculiar difficulties to the investigator because of their inherent intricacies and complexities. These subtle, ever-changing, and ever-growing processes of the psychical world are evidently not to be attacked by the methods which a scientist adopts to investigate the simple and palpable facts relating to lifeless objects and organisms of lower orders. In such cases varying methods have to be adopted to suit the complex facts relating to each class of human phenomena. And when the truths thus separately discovered have been verified and methodized, the knowledge about man approaches a perfection and system really deserving the name of science.

The facts and phenomena of the

human world are always changing their ground ; they are never at standstill. The human mind is progressive, and the faculties of man attain a many-sided and varied development. And so there is no fixity and stationariness in human affairs and institutions. Every moment a new is taking the place of the old, and thus a " history " is being made ; and on account of such incessant changes history never repeats itself, but displays novel types and situations at every stage. Systems of philosophy and ideals of life and thought as well as of literature and science are constantly shifting their positions of equilibrium. Human civilization is, in fact, a dynamic process, a living, moving, and continuously developing phenomenon with a peculiar history of its own.

Our end will be defeated if we inquire into any one phase or stage of social life. For such a statical study reveals the condition of civilization at only one stage of its existence. To acquire a full knowledge of a running stream one has to traverse its whole length. If, however, one places himself at a particular spot on its bank, one cannot hope to know of the thousand and one wanderings and the varying characteristics of the different situations before it reaches its goal. One must walk with the stream to know it fully. Similarly, to appreciate the growth and development of the human mind and understand in its entirety the stream of human civilization which has had a gradual growth and evolution we must not confine ourselves to a single chapter or phase or study only certain types of life and culture, but must place ourselves in the midst of the varieties and diversities that have characterized human civilization in its different epochs and seats.

The historical inquiry is thus the apt method of investigating social phenomena and the proper foundation of the sciences about man. The thoughts and actions of men in different times and places are the materials out of which to construct a systematic and coherent human science. That certainly is a very incomplete and imperfect knowledge about man which gives us no conception of the varieties of human ideals in institutions and languages, and diversities of political and social theories and organizations. Such knowledge as does not supply one with the types of human culture and differences in the standpoints and objectives of man under the different sets of circumstances is quite useless for practical purposes of advice and guidance in the actual world. For here all institutions and suggestions have to be adapted to the particular conditions of each case.

Thus, for example, if we want to build up Sciences and Arts about wealth and property and, generally speaking, about the wants and enjoyments of man, we should try to collect materials for a history of human wants and enjoyments and the various stages in the evolution of property. For in different ages and at different places the wants and activities of man have assumed different shapes and given rise to different socio-economic and industrial institutions. And these institutions have been the outcome of man's varying conceptions about things temporal and spiritual and the ideals regulating his whole life and conduct in the universe. In this way, Status and Contract, Domestic System and Factory System, Trade Unions and Joint Stock Companies, Direct Dealing and Middlemen's Interventions, Barter and Money, have diversified the economic history of civilization. Hence Economic Science cannot be founded on the study of facts and phenomena of only one stage of man's economic evolution, and the generalizations that are based on materials adapted to only one type of institutions and ideals must necessarily be unscientific, partial, and erroneous.

The same may be said of religion. The ultimate truth about religion and man's religious conceptions and the laws about the growth and development of religious sense in man cannot be arrived at from an account of only one isolated stage of human society, from a description of the religious ideals and institutions that characterize only one age in the history of civilization. So also in order that we may get a clear idea of the elements of literature, the conditions and criteria of literary perfection and the laws of growth and expansion of literature, the connection between literature and national ideals, we have to study the literary and linguistic facts and phenomena not of any one epoch in human history but of several types of literary life and institutions that have diversified the history of literature in the world.

But though the human mind is

essentially progressive and the law of perpetual flux is the fundamental truth about human ideals and institutions, so that varieties and diversities are the natural phenomena of the world of human beings, yet there are certain deep-seated characteristics which are common to all times and all ages, that are permanent and universal ingredients of human nature itself. These essentially human characteristics are what differentiate man from the rest of the created world. These supply the fundamental unity and basal uniformity pervading the whole human society—underlying the thousand and one differences and types of physical and mental outfit. They are the never-changing and stationary elements of human character.

Man has thus twofold characteristics. In the first place, he is ever-moving, ever-varying. In the second place, he is fixed and permanent: he does not know change and motion. To grapple with this double nature of man the scientist has to use a double machinery—the dynamic as well as static.

Thus the human sciences are amenable to two methods of investigation, viz.: (1) The historical method, which deals with facts furnished by History, the record of changes and movements in civilization; and (2) the Philosophical method, which exhibits the fixed and permanent characteristics of human life and civilization, unities and uniformities of ideals. Each method by itself leads only to partial and one-sided truths; so in the interest of the whole truth we have to use both the methods. If we restrict our inquiry to a particular stage of human society we fail to perceive continuous growth and development, the series of vicissitudes that constitute the life and soul of civilization. But until and unless we devote special attention also to a study of the facts and phenomena of a certain fixed stage in its history, of one of the conditions of its Stable Equilibrium, we lose sight of the eternal truths and permanent principles underlying human nature and civilization—the essential and universal characteristics of man.

For though, no doubt, widely different forms of organization have come into existence in different parts of the world, there are certain common characteristics of human nature which have made man essentially a gregarious and political animal, and which have left their stamp upon all the varying types of social organization. Analyse the human mind and the very nature of man or his society at any one of its stages, and facts will at once be disclosed as to whether the association between man and man is indispensable or whether he can supply all his wants independently of others' help. No historical inquiry is necessary for such an investigation. The study of one man is the study of all. Similarly, such questions as the utility of Literature, its inception and its influence, and its connection with human mind, may be solved by an inquiry into the facts and phenomena of literary history at any one of its stages. So also the economic and religious elements ever present in the human nature, if analysed, may furnish a sound basis of knowledge about socio - religious and socio - economic ideals and institutions. Thus historical evidences and the study of varieties may be dispensed with, and an investigation into the essential characteristics of any human being or any one society of men may be substituted for them when the object is to explain such questions as to why men pray, why they establish temples, why they follow doctrines and study religious books; or why arts and industries were invented and why the institutions of property came into being or why economic organizations are necessary.

SECTION II

DIVISIONS OF PEDAGOGICS

(i) Historical.

BOTH the historical and the philosophical methods must, therefore, be combined for the establishment of the science of education. The investigation of such pedagogic problems as the meaning of education, its necessity, its objects and its contents, its influences on the human mind and general principles or universal rules, if any, for the guidance and control of education, requires this twofold study.

The science of education has consequently to be divided into two distinct branches. In the first place, we have to describe the principal educational systems that have been established in different ages to meet the varying needs of societies. In describing each system we shall discuss the lines of education and the theories of educators, the aims and objects of the educational body as well as the ideals of the society. We shall try to get some idea of the position of the teacher in society, and the relation between the student and the teacher; we shall also have to explain such topics as to how the subjects for study were chosen and what means were adopted to impart moral, political, and religious instruction. The governmental or administrative questions regarding educational management, and control, have, moreover, to be considered in addition to the discussion of the methods of teaching adopted and the pedagogic machinery and apparatus used. An account of the educational systems of the world will thus furnish us with the various chapters in its history and the different stages of social evolution.

In this way we propose to give a brief sketch of the educational ideals and practices of the Hindus, Greeks, and Egyptians of the ancient times, as well as to study the pedagogic systems of Europe in the Middle Ages and to survey the chief universities of the modern world. This history of education will not, however, be treated in a chronological order, but according to the different ideals of education followed by each nation. Our object will thus be to describe some of the principal landmarks and only the chief types of educational organizations of the world, and thus present some of the specimens of human civilization; and not to give a full history of the educational systems that represent the successive stages in the cultural growth and evolution of Mankind.

(ii) PHILOSOPHICAL.

The historical inquiry will be supplemented by a philosophical investigation. Such questions as the following demand answer in this branch of pedagogics, viz., What is education? What is the influence of education upon human mind? Is there an ideally best system of education? What are the theories of education? Why do changes in the system of education become indispensable with alterations in the conditions of society? Are the varieties in educational ideals and systems justified?

The philosophical method will vindicate the varieties in educational systems and types of educational policies revealed by history. The discovery of the particular system of education that is specially adapted to the nature and requirements of the people of this country will, of course, be the function of the philosophical method. For the need of special arrangements for special circumstances and the relativity of each educational ideal to the conditions of life and thought to which it has to adapt itself are the basic truths of this method of inquiry.

Human Life a Process of Natural

Development.—Man is born with an endowment of certain powers and faculties. These powers and faculties grow and develop naturally under the influence of the surrounding forces of the world. The forces and powers of nature, the objects in the physical world, the society, the State, and various other institutions of civilization are the factors that go to make the whole environment of man, and spontaneously help in forming the character of childhood and youth. The moulding of life and habits and the growth of personality and individuality are natural processes which go on even if unaided by any special arrangements made for the unfolding of men's latent aptitudes and capabilities. Constituted as man is, he is constantly drawing his sustenance and materials for the building up of his physique and manhood from the physical and social world without. It is the characteristic of a living being to utilize in this way the forces of nature and assimilate the products of the environment with one's own characteristics.

Education a Help to this Life-Building Process. — Education is nothing but the comprehensive means of helping forward this natural life-process. It is an aid to the manifestation and display of vital energy, and accelerates the spontaneous development of individuality through the assimilation of the forces and materials in the universe. It is a process by which the individual and the environment are brought into relation with one another in the interests of the individual's life and progress.

Educational Institutions must therefore Help Forward the Same Process.—If, then, it is necessary that some ways and means must be devised by man for the proper development of his mental and physical faculties, the ways and means must have to follow this spontaneous process of life-building and the lines of its natural development. If it is at all necessary and desirable to establish an institution for educational purposes, the suitability of such an institution must be taken into consideration by having reference to the social, political, and religious conditions of the people for whom it is intended. For the life and development of the people have been already adjusted to those surrounding circumstances. If these factors in the existing and past conditions of its national growth are neglected by the responsible guardians of society while formulating schemes of education, the healthy progress of life's development along normal and natural lines will be retarded, and in the place of easily growing specimens of humanity the world will witness the rise of an abnormal and degenerate society of human beings. And such results are the very things to be avoided and prevented by educational arrangements, for they run counter to the very ends and objects of education, viz., the development of the individual along the lines of his own natural evolution.

Corollaries to the Doctrine of Natural Development.—But since vital processes and conditions of natural development are not uniform, but vary with peoples in different ages and countries, it follows that educational institutions must be very varied in character and ideals. Regard must therefore be paid to time, place, and circumstances for the building up of educational institutions. The system of education must vary with the varying conditions in the environment. Every place must have its own pedagogics, every age also must have its own. The good old rules may prove effete in an altered condition of society. The medicine of a people under one set of circumstances may be poison under another: "The old order changeth, yielding place to new," "lest one good custom should corrupt the world." If the system of education does not keep pace with the changes in social conditions the system becomes antiquated, loses its up-to-dateness and adaptability, and hence becomes quite unfit as a means to the further development of the people. The arrangements become vitiated, pervert the faculties of the individuals, and arrest their growth by preventing them from taking advantage of the forces of the surrounding world for their own nurture and development. The senses of man are thus stunted and dwarfed even as flowers artificially blossomed in a hot-house or exotics in an alien soil.

If, again, we must profit by our environment and utilize its gifts for our own growth, we must have the opportunity to turn them to our account, free and unobstructed; and sufficient latitude must be afforded for the free play of our faculties. If one does not get scope for independent action, assimilation of world-forces and development along normal lines are greatly hindered and may become wellnigh impossible. The reason is, a man is responsible for his own culture; the individual peculiarities of a man are best known to himself; others can have only a conjecture of them. And so indeed, if anybody is ever entrusted with the authority of building up another man's ideals, the censor or the curator can only perform his duties conscientiously by keeping in view the peculiar characteristics of the person concerned. The guide will have to plan his work by accepting and recognizing the independence and individuality of the latter, and in such a way as to promote that freedom and separateness.

Such Institutions as Help Forward the Process of Natural Development are called " National." — Whenever, therefore, a system of education has to be promulgated, the organizers must hit upon that which is adapted to the character and requirements of the people for whom it is intended, and is modern and up to date according to the latest developments of the time. The genius of the nation, its historic individuality, the type of culture it has evolved, its ideals in actual life and traditions, on the one hand; and, on the other, the spirit of the age, *i.e.*, the highest and the best truths discovered and realized by the other members of the human society at the time, the accumulated experience and culture of humanity, and the lines of its possible development in the immediate and remote future, must be taken into consideration by the educational organizers of every age and clime. Such a system of education as is based on a due calculation of these forces may be called the natural or national system. This national system will thus be peculiarly adapted to a particular country in a particular age; and while it does fulfil its present necessity, it also prepares the way for its future development, and thus indirectly contributes to the richness of world's civilization and progress.

In the first place, anybody who attempts to stick to the good old rules, when they are unsuitable, forcibly attempts only an impossible task; and therefore these are to be forsaken in the interests of the people's natural growth at the proper time. But, in the second place, the conditions of natural development as conduced to by national education require also that the hoary past must by no means be forgotten, for then we should be trying to build a house on sands. The aims and objects, therefore, of the organizers of the natural and therefore national system of education must be, first, to attach a special importance to the study of the nation's ideals and achievements in arts, literature, and sciences, so as to imbue the learner with the best and noblest ideas of his community, past and present, and make him realize his oneness with the great whole of collective national life; and, in the second place, to build up, on the substructure of national sentiments and as an aid to their further development, the culture of universal humanity, so as to incorporate with the varied traditions of the nation the best assimilable ideals of civilized mankind.

Freedom, Race-tradition, and Modernity are thus the three principal features of the national system of education. Having described this system in its general and theoretical aspects in the second branch of pedagogics, viz., that based on the philosophical method of inquiry, we shall suggest the system that is conducive to the best interests of the people of of this country and possesses all the characteristics of "national education" as discussed above.

A scheme of education will be worked out that is calculated to help forward the natural and ingrained characteristics of the Indian people along the paths of progress, as well as to meet the pressing needs of the community at the present time. And in connection with the picture of a modern national system adapted to the requirements of India, all such topics as the arrangements for moral and religious training, the period and hours of work, the establishment of institutions, the curriculum of studies, the relation between the teacher and the pupil, and other pedagogic questions regarding a university, will, of course, be discussed.

(iii) Practical—Art of Teaching.

Sciences have two aspects—positive or theoretical, and practical or applied. As a positive study, science confines itself to the investigation of the facts and phenomena, as they are and have been, how they happen, their inter-connections and inter-dependences. The theoretical investigator pursues his analysis and synthesis of the topics without any end in view—solely for themselves—to get at the truths about them. He has no concern with the ethical or utilitarian considerations affecting his studies.

But the other aspect of science concerns itself with the ends to be derived and the objects that may possibly be realized by pursuing the research. As an applied or practical study, science has certain definite aims to further and has to devise ways and means for their fulfilment. The investigator is not merely satisfied with the knowledge of the processes and the abstract truths regarding the phenomena; his chief concern is the uses to which the truths may be applied and the work that may be done with them.

One part of science merely discovers

principles and laws and establishes truths, the other applies those rules to practical purposes and actually ministers to social well-being. The two together form a complete science. Disinterested and dispassionate investigation of truths by the philosophical and historical methods without any distinct end in view, as well as the invention of means and methods to fulfil certain ends, are the two functions of scientists. The latter of these functions stands upon the former, inasmuch as it is the positive knowledge of the truth about a matter that furnishes a basis for the practical man, and inadequate information is of very little help in guiding the actual course of an action. And so the applied sciences are based on the positive.

Economics has thus two branches. As a positive science it furnishes us with the laws and general principles of the production, distribution, consumption, and exchange of wealth without in any way suggesting changes in the socio-economic institutions or remarking on the justice or legitimacy of certain classes of economic phenomena. As an applied science or art, however, economics has an ideal or goal to attain—justice, equality, increase of well-being, augmentation of national wealth, etc., and as such has to discuss the methods by which those ends may be promoted. The practical economist has to pronounce judgments and dictate rules.

In like manner political science as a theoretical study investigates such political facts and phenomena as the origin, development, downfall, and extinction of states, international diplomacy, constitutional growths, relations between rulers and ruled, etc., and formulates general principles that have regulated the activities and thoughts of men as members of society in all ages and countries and are likely to influence them so long as man is man. But political science has an applied or practical branch also, called the art of politics, which dictates rules that must be carried out by actual administrators, legislators, and financiers in the interest of the good and sound government of a state. The principles of political science have to be applied by the politicians and officers of the state in the administration of government.

The science of education, like every

other science, has the same twofold aspect. In the first place, by the historical and philosophical studies, the nature, scope, ideals, and means of education have to be discovered. This is the positive or theoretical aspect of pedagogics. It investigates the principles and ideals underlying all educational systems of the world, the causes of their variety, and their connection with literature and other aspects of national life; and studies the nature of the human mind, the laws of its growth and development, the instruments that help the process of its unfolding, the various stages of human life, and the likes and dislikes in each.

In the second place, pedagogics is also a practical science. As such it devises measures for the utilization of the principles regarding the growth of civilization and the development of man's body and mind in the practical interests of the individual's strength and efficiency; and discovers methods and formulates rules by which a people can be equipped in the struggle for existence. It advises man to seek certain forces in the environment, and reject certain others, and use them according to certain methods, and thus helps forward his attempts at self-culture and progress. Educationists cannot rest content by simply pointing out the connection between the current civilization and the system of education; nor are they satisfied by simply describing the processes of education, the causes of its progress and decay. Nor, again, is the work of the educationists finished by simply narrating how educational ideals are influenced by the spirit of the age and environment and suggesting changes in the system of education. They have, over and above, to suggest a method of teaching and learning the subjects of study in the most profitable and practical way.

Educationists have thus a threefold function, and thus the science of education has to be divided into three distinct branches:—(i) System of education. (ii) Theory of education. (iii) Art of education.

The first of these divisions treats of the varieties in the educational organizations of the world. The second will explain the origin of this variety by a philosophical discussion of the theory and nature of education, and establish the truth that educational institutions and policies must necessarily be diverse because of the diversity of the peoples in needs, temperaments, and characteristics. In this book will be advanced the plea for separate educational organizations adapted to the requirements of Indian life. The third division of pedagogics will address itself to the devising of ways and means for the carrying out of the theory propounded by the philosophical discussion in the second branch.

Thus, in the first place, the scheme of an educational organization, with all its paraphernalia, machinery, and apparatus, will be discussed. In the second place, the scheme of an organization suited to Indian requirements will be devised, and the arrangements for physical, mental, and religious training, the control and discipline of students, the regulation of university life, and other necessary things will be described. And in the third place, a special method of teaching will be suggested which is likely to combine economy of time and labour with efficiency and pleasure. But of these three classes of problems comprised within the third division of pedagogics —*i.e.* the art of education—the first two I propose to dispose of towards the close of the second division, *i.e.* that treating of the philosophy of education. So the whole of the third division will confine itself to the remaining aspect of the practical branch, viz., the elaboration of the art of teaching the various subjects.

SECTION III

THE INDUCTIVE METHOD OF TEACHING

A THOROUGH change will have to be made in the art of education that obtains currency in this country in the interest of the comprehensive scheme of an altogether new method of teaching. To speak briefly, the method to be inaugurated is such as enables the student to proceed from the known to the unknown according to the various stages of the development of his manhood, and confers on him the pleasure of actively exercising his own powers of observation and experiment at every step. The new method is calculated to enable the learner to enjoy the blessings of his intellectual gifts and constructive faculties as a human being, and realize his position as a discoverer and creator. This method will make him appreciate his own original ways of thinking and perceive the individuality of his intellectual life by introducing him not only to the truths to be learnt but simultaneously also to the methods and processes of discovering them. And it will arrange the subjects of study and topics for discussion in such an order of sequence and coexistence as is suited to the growth of man's mental faculties and the development of his powers of assimilation.

The scientist trudges through the *terra incognita* of his field of discovery by slow steps, and at every point he has got to struggle with many an obscure untruth that sometimes bewilders and defeats him. He can arrive at some sort of working hypothesis only after the collection of many seeming and partial truths as the result of his diverse investigations into the unknown. These hypotheses and half-truths, the products of the several stages of conflict between light and darkness, human effort and the resistance of Nature, constitute a long and tedious series which may ultimately lead to the discovery of the final truths. The student has likewise to wade through the realm of knowledge with uncertain steps, encountering difficulties and overcoming them at every turn. He should follow the practice of the scientific discoverer, and be prepared for a thousand and one failures in acquiring mastery over a certain subject.

The duty of the teacher is not to force upon the students, and make them memorize, the truths that had been discovered by others. He has solely to guide and assist them like a pioneer in their attempts to obtain knowledge at first hand and discover truths in their own ways.

But there is certainly a difference between a scientific discoverer and a learner. The one has nobody to guide him, but has to grope absolutely in the dark, and has necessarily to undergo many unnecessary and fruitless troubles. It is the silent and disinterested performance of such thankless tasks by many "mute inglorious" workers that has prepared the way for a single discovery; and as a consequence a good deal of human energy has to be wasted for nothing. But the learner will be subjected to no such fruitless labour. There is for him the accumulated treasure of science and philosophy earned by the combined effort of different races and individuals; and there is his assistant, the teacher, who has in his possession the key that would unlock this treasury and is the master of its contents. The student need not discover over again the methods by which investigators have arrived at the truths, for they are all known to his guide, who is constantly watching his progress and helping him with suggestions in need. And so he can acquire easily and in a short time what was achieved by the world in many generations. There is little danger of a student's life being a total failure like the life of many a learned scholar and scientific explorer.

Thus the pupil must not be a mere reader, he must be a discoverer and creator too. The young learner need not exactly follow the lines of research or blindly imitate the methods of investigation adopted by the writers and authors of books. The method of studying a subject is to be quite different from the method of writing a book. The books do not contain an account of the efforts and endeavours of the author, do not indicate the ways and means of investigation, and do not describe how a solution was arrived at. The authors try to put down, cut and dried, in an ordered and systematic form their thoughts and ideas on a certain subject, the results of multifarious researches into it, and comparisons with the established truths and opinions about it. The attempt at systematizing makes books consequential and logical indeed, but this art of book-making, while serving very well the purpose of books as books, does not suit the requirements of the student; for to him the process of working out a problem is more important than the solution of the problem itself.

Even the books of learned authors are incapable of giving such help as the students require, and hence should not be used by them. Of course there are various reasons for which students should know thoroughly the contents of works by standard authors and their methods of presenting a subject and dealing with a topic. But the general rule of teaching should be not to introduce the pupil to any books except only such as are peculiarly calculated to suit the purpose of learners and specially made for their use, and not written as standard books embodying the products of any investigation. Books that compel the students to exercise their own faculties according to their capacities, books that are suggestive without being exhaustive, are the only ones, if at all, that can be recommended to and may be studied by the students under the supervision of teachers.

The study of a subject in accordance with the method of discovery necessarily involves freedom and originality of thinking, fosters the spirit of inquiry, and develops the capacity for self-exertion. Students brought up in this method will give unmistakable indication of free thinking, self-help, originality, and inquisitiveness. This exercise of brain at one's own initiative quickens the intellect and rouses its powers; since exercise develops the faculties, and the powers of the mind grow and develop when they have to grapple with difficulties. The student must not therefore stuff his memory with the second-hand knowledge derived from books written by others, but should try to clear up the difficulties that he comes across while studying a particular subject.

Of the various methods of discovery, *i.e.*, proceeding from the known to the unknown, the learner should use that which necessitates the investigation of a great variety of facts and phenomena. The ultimate object would be to systematize and methodize the results of these individual investigations and find out the unity in the diversity and the general principle underlying the varied instances. This method of inquiry, by which one ascends from the individual to the general, particular to the common, concrete to the abstract, is called the inductive method. It affords a sound basis of facts for knowledge to strike its roots deep down. It compels the student to be an original thinker, who has his own responsibility to discover a path, by creating for him sufficient opportunities for making independent use of his own brain, and endows him with the scientific spirit of inquiry, the taste for seeking truths by habituating him to the analysis and synthesis of innumerable facts and events of the universe.

This method attaches special importance to the known facts, which are to be used as the basis, the data for discoveries and generalizations. Unknown facts must not be learned by rote from the teacher. There will be a predominance of object-lessons and the study of facts and concrete things in a method like this. The student will have to acquire principles and general rules after the long and tedious analysis of individual cases. This method will demand of the student in the initial stages an intimacy with the materials and events that are close at hand and hence familiar, and subsequently with the growth of his intelligence and imagination, the observation and study of distant, unfamiliar, and past or future facts and phenomena. Imagination based on reason will carry him gradually from the sphere of known facts to the region of unknown, and secrets of past and future will then be revealed to his eyes. By gradual steps the student will advance from simple to complex truths, and from the concrete facts to subtle and abstract generalizations or principles.

SECTION IV

THE STUDY OF LANGUAGES

IN order to attain mastery over the languages we must adopt the same method by which we learn our mother-tongue. In the first instance the babbling child tries to express at least one simple idea. It is this expression of ideas to others and the development of his power of expression that give him gradually a command over the resources of his language and literature ; and the necessity of expressing many intricate ideas according to the varied wants of life makes his expression manifold and complex.

Now, one solitary word can scarcely express an idea. A complete sense, a full thought is represented by only the sentence. The sentence may be very short, it may consist of two words only, but it is the sentence that is the only vehicle of communication and interchange of ideas. The sentence must therefore be used as the unit of language; and the student must try from the very beginning to compose sentences in the language which he wants to learn. While practising to compose sentences he should learn how to avoid the errors and wrong uses as well as correct the mistakes committed by others. The learner should be placed in such situations in which he must try to express himself in that language and hold frequent conversations with those to whom that is the mother-tongue.

In short, any language to be learnt

should be regarded as the mother-tongue.

Grammar as such may be dispensed with in picking up a language and studying its literature. The rules of grammar are of course learnt imperceptibly by students while composing sentences and actually using the language. But though grammar has to be learnt as an independent science, as preparatory to the study of philology and the logic of languages, no preliminary or concomitant training in the rules, generalizations, and definitions of grammar is necessary for learning the language itself.

SECTION V

THE STUDY OF HISTORY

WE have seen that the familiar method of picking up the mother-tongue by conversation and actual use of sentences to convey ideas is to be adopted in learning the other languages. So also the knowledge of the familiar contemporary national history should be used as the basis of all historical studies.

The knowledge of man about the universe grows and expands round self-knowledge,—the knowledge about one's identity, continuity, and individuality as the centre and nucleus of all truths. It is the perception of self that is the foundation of all other perceptions, that makes observation of, and inferences about, non-self possible. It is by placing the external *objects* in contact with the *subject*, *i.e.*, one's own self, by comparing and contrasting the self with the non-self and realizing the relations of one's own body and mind with the surrounding environment, both physical and human, that man acquires and develops his intelligence and thinking powers.

Hence the study and examination of the surrounding objects and events should follow and be grafted on intimacy and familiarity with the life and thought-processes of the individual self. A student of history must not therefore trouble himself with the account of remote ages and of foreign peoples at the outset. He should attend first to those factors of national life, those familiar facts and phenomena of society in the making of which he himself lends his active help. The universe of thought and action which is actually bound up with the learner's own life and experiences, which is being constantly modified and built up by the thoughts and activities of himself, and of those whom he knows most, should be the object of the beginner's study and the "radicle" of his further progress in history.

If a student has opportunity of placing himself amidst and observing the complex social, political, economic, and religious movements of his own days, and of studying changes that are being effected therein, he can easily realize that every man by his thoughts and activities is a maker of his society's history and is shaping the destiny of his nation; and the conception dawns upon him that history is a living, growing, and moving science, and is the study of vital processes, and living and expanding thoughts, and not of mechanical forces or dead substances. Such a study of concrete and living facts and materials of national life will impress him with the similarity of life that exists between the ancient and the modern peoples and of those who are to come. This enables the learner to realize the fact that the actors on the stage of past or foreign history were men of real flesh and blood like those of the present epoch, that the industrial, political, and social movements of the modern times have their prototype in the ancient world, and that there is nothing extraordinary in the records of societies distant in time or space. History studied in this method makes a deep impression upon the mind of the learner.

The different stages of the evolution of human civilization and the fundamental laws of progress as explained by the science of history are extremely subtle, and the comprehension of these scientific principles requires a vigorous exercise of the reasoning and imaginative faculty. To arrive at such a philosophy of history should be the ultimate aim and goal of historical studies. But to a beginner these subtle and abstract truths seem to be rather unreal, imaginary, and metaphysical. So it is the events and facts, incidents and movements out of which those subtle generalizations can be deduced, the data of the science of history, and not the abstract principles and inferences, that should form the subject of the very first lessons in history.

The learner must direct his attention to the concrete facts and institutions of civilization and the factors of national life, *e.g.*, language, literature, philosophy, arts, industry, politics, and religion of the country, and thus familiarize himself with the living forces that go to form the history of a people. He need not at the outset attend to the relations of cause and effect that subsist between the several constituents of national life or between it and the surrounding environments, or to the laws of growth and development of the social organism. The student must first understand the forces underlying the events that surround him and make up his world of thought and action. He may then compare the past with the present and study it in the light of the present. He will thus acquire a thorough knowledge of his national history, and this will enable him to institute a comparison between the characteristics of his own civilization and those of other nations.

The student of history should thus ascend from the present to the past and through the national to the universal on the principle of comparing new acquisitions with the old and adding them to the existing stock. This method of study gives the student a sufficient grasp of the forces that go to form the life of a people. The student can in this way understand the position of his own country in the scale of nations, and can effectively master the principles underlying the gradual evolution of civilization and the law regulating the progress of humanity.

SECTION VI

THE STUDY OF GEOGRAPHY

GEOGRAPHY is the "physical basis" of the historical science, and history is imperfect without geography. As the mind has its basis of operations in the body, so also this physical world is the stage on which the human beings play their parts. Imperfect will be our knowledge of human life and society if we neglect to study the natural surroundings and the physical environments which to a great extent regulate and govern the character of the field of human habitation and activity. A knowledge of geography as the science of these physical agencies is thus preliminary to the study of the activities of men.

In geography as in history we must proceed from the known to the unknown, the familiar to the unfamiliar, the near to the distant. The geography of our native land must first attract our attention. If we are ignorant of the rivers, forests, plants, animals, industries, trade, and commerce of our mother country we cannot expect to have a living conception of the physical and geographical characteristics of other countries, for it is only by reference to one's own self, to the existing stock of ideas, by *apperception* as it is called, that our knowledge becomes real, effective, and living.

In order that one may receive and entertain guests and offer hospitality to strangers one should be a householder and have a "home." If, however, one has no local habitation, no centre of affection, no fixed points round which to group associations and ideas, even a most diversely varied life and the experiences of many lands and peoples cannot leave him wiser and more informed, for these cannot stay, but vanish as soon as they rise.

The concrete geographical forces and features should demand the attention of the student in the beginning. Such abstruse truths as those regarding the influence of environment upon society or the reaction of Man upon Nature must not be discussed by the beginner. He should rather equip himself with a sound knowledge of the physical characteristics of his motherland and other countries in the order of importance or of social, political, or natural connections. In doing so the student of geography should gather information about the lithosphere, hydrosphere, and atmosphere of the various regions of the globe, *i.e.*, about those natural agencies and physical forces in land, water, air, etc., that influence a nation's social, political, and religious institutions, and that govern the economic resources of a country. A knowledge of concrete and familiar things that lie about him will gradually lead him to the discovery of the subtle principles of geography as a science of the physical forces of the universe.

SECTION VII

THE STUDY OF MENTAL AND MORAL SCIENCES

THE method of studying the historical science is to be applied to the other human sciences also, *e.g.*, Logic, Ethics, Economics, Politics, Psychology, and Sociology. The subject matter of these sciences is human mind and character—the ideals and institutions of man, and as such is very complex and intricate.

On account of the complexities and ramifications inherent in the mental and moral phenomena, these sciences have an abstract subtlety and a metaphysical character peculiar to themselves. The method of proceeding from the concrete to the abstract and the familiar to the unfamiliar is, therefore, specially necessary in mastering these sciences. The mental processes and products, facts and phenomena of the moral world, economic institutions and organizations, political and social movements, are the concrete materials — the data of the human and social sciences that should first demand attention. Generalizations have to be deduced out of them, universal principles enunciated in subsequent stages after a careful analysis of the individual cases and comparison and contrast between them. Not the laws but the facts, not "general" principles but "particular" events of mental and moral life, the affairs of the economic and political world, are to be regarded as the proper subjects of study.

Instead of taking a few facts and isolated events as illustrations of the principles, those events and facts should be the primary topics for discussion and study; and the principles should be gradually drawn from them as subsidiary and auxiliary. The universal principles and the highest generalizations of the human sciences have to be deduced in this way out of the concrete world of the "particular" human and social phenomena.

Thus, to arrive at the laws underlying the operations of the human mind, the connections between the various classes of mental phenomena and the psychological growth of man, the student must be well grounded in a knowledge of the diverse thought-processes and emotional and volitional conditions of man; and analyse and compare the multifarious sensations, perceptions, conceptions, judgments, decisions, affections, and desires that go to make up his psychical life. These diverse mental experiences are the materials of the science of psychology, and the learner should thoroughly familiarize himself with this diversity and variety in order that he may have a sound preparation and adequate equipment for the "unities" and "common" principles.

The student of ethics should likewise equip himself with a knowledge of those instances of human conduct which are generally described as right, and those which are condemned as having infringed on the rules of morality. In order that he may come to a correct view regarding the rightness and wrongness of things, the true standard of judgment and the principles that should regulate human actions, the student must be well grounded in concrete specimens of sins and virtues and the ideals underlying men's everyday judgment of things and events.

Similarly the student of the science of the "regulative principles of thought" should begin with an account of various specimens of right thinking and fallacious reasonings, instances of good argumentation and lunatic, inconsistent, or irrational statements, and should acquire a knowledge of the various standards by which people in everyday life judge of human thoughts as correct or erroneous. When the number of cases is sufficiently large he will be in a position to compare the correct with the incorrect, and the truth with the untruth, and master the general principles on which men's conceptions of right and wrong thinking are based.

Again, the actual manners, customs, and usages of various peoples, their rites and ceremonies, must receive the student's fullest consideration if he wants to discover the *spirit* that underlies them. To the student of sociology the facts and phenomena of social life, the institutions and practices through which man displays his inner nature and spiritual characteristics, have the greatest importance.

Economics should be learnt by observing the various institutions of property and industrial organization that come into being in different ages in different countries. In this connection a close examination of the industries, arts, trade and, commerce must be resorted to, and the facts and phenomena of the production, distribution, consumption, and exchange of wealth and all such concrete incidents as make up the material life of a people should be studied by the beginner. He should finally generalize these occurrences of everyday economic life into principles of economic science.

Political science also has to be mastered by observing the real political events and the actual incidents of constitutional life of a people, and by comparing highly advanced political societies with fallen nations. A preliminary discussion of the various forms of constitution and governmental machinery as well as of the political events of the past and present in this connection is indispensable to students of political science. They should also analyse the causes of conflict between self-interest and national interest as well as conflicts between nation and nation, and study the many solutions that have been arrived at in history by treaties, charters, and conferences.

Moral, spiritual, political, and economical questions arise in the communal, social, political, and other spheres of every individual's life. These questions of the human world give rise to problems of truth and falsehood, good and evil, religion and irreligion, progression and retrogression, profit and loss, war and peace, amity and enmity, victory and defeat, respect and insult. Solutions of such universal problems have been attempted by all men in their lives. Accounts of revolution and evolution embodied in history throw light upon these questions, and poets and dramatists have essayed to answer these questions through their art according to their capacity and inclination. It is these problems of human life that the students of philosophy should grapple with and analyse and dissect in order to discover ultimately the laws underlying the multifarious occurrences of the human world. The student should be well up in the facts and master and marshal them well before he undertakes in his own way to explain or account for them and discover their causal relations.

The student's attention is drawn to

the fundamental elements and the basic foundations of language, history, geography, philosophy, economics, and politics, when these literary subjects or arts, as they are generally called, are studied according to the inductive method. By being always in touch with the concrete data of the human sciences, the historical, philosophical, and literary faculties of the student are properly exercised and receive their adequate development.

This method may also be adopted with considerable advantage in the study of mathematics and natural sciences; it affords opportunities to the students for the development of their mathematical sense and the creation of an interest in original research. The inductive method as described above adequately sets at work those faculties of the mind by the exercise of which mathematics can be mastered and a desire for questioning Nature is generated.

SECTION VIII

THE STUDY OF MATHEMATICS

ACCORDING to the prevalent method of teaching mathematics the student is presented with a number of lifeless digits; and numbers, digits, signs as well as arithmetic, algebra, and geometry seem to have their existence only on paper or on board. They thus lack the influence which living truths can have on human minds. For things with which human life has very little and only a remote connection fail to create any living interest in them. Occasionally the teacher, for the purpose of importing an amount of lively interest into the subject, draws a diagram or refers to some actual event with a view to solve a difficult problem; but this much is scarcely sufficient to evoke that interest in the mind of students which can impel him to pursue the subject with keen attention or generate a genuine devotion to it.

The method that is being suggested in these pages will make the mathematical subjects vivid and inspiring by bringing them within the purview of daily avocations and the circle of human interests. Men have daily to count many things, weigh many things, and measure many things. To such familiar incidents of daily life the attention of the student should be directed. From time immemorial measurements of time, lengths, and weights have been common occurrences in the material life of nations.

These universal practices are intimately connected with trade, commerce, arts, and industries, and with the origin and evolution of private property. It follows from this that a knowledge of these subjects will necessarily lead to the knowledge of the mathematical elements involved in and mixed up with them. Man is by nature an economic animal, and he has been mathematical ever since he has been economic. Economics and mathematics, material life and calculations, go hand in hand. And so mathematics should be learnt not as an abstract science but as having a vital connection with man's economic practices. By being thus brought into connection with the problems of human life, mathematics can be made living, attractive, and interesting. The student can feel inspired in mathematics only if it be presented in the form of problems and questions associated with the losses and gains, interests and profits, divisions and augmentations of property which men enjoy. Otherwise it is a dry, husky, unsentimental, and abstruse subject which is likely to scare away many young minds.

The student will have to be introduced to the various problems that can possibly arise regarding the measurable world. Commercial dealings, profit and loss, giving and taking of debts, buying and selling, partition and exchange, are some of the subjects relating to wealth and involving practical mathematical questions. These problems engross the greater part of human life. These and many others, therefore, are the subjects to be learnt by the student of mathematics. He should be asked to solve problems of measurement regarding these economic incidents of human life.

All those affairs of human life which have concern with the transactions affecting property, industry, and commerce are extremely complex and intricate in their nature. Co-operative enterprise, joint-stock business, banking, collection of revenue, internal and international trade are difficult transactions and demand a good deal of business intelligence and financial statesmanship for their proper administration. The student, however, will acquire a good knowledge of mathematics if he attends only to those economico-mathematical problems that are comparatively easy and simple in calculation.

In the interest of the proper development of the mathematical faculties, the learner need not grapple with "Asses' Bridges" and "hard knots," but should be habituated to working out such problems as do not require very great mental strain or hard and tedious calculations or involve long and troublesome processes.

The student should be encouraged to answer mathematical questions orally without the aid of signs, numbers, or letters. It is not at all necessary to have recourse to cumbrous sums to understand and master mathematics. Without increasing the complexity of signs and figures and by introducing the smallest and simplest number one can learn all the principles involved in the calculations and measurements that may be possibly necessary to man in life. By these simple devices the most difficult problem can be rendered easy of treatment and solution. The ability to work out hard exercises and solve intricate problems is not the surest indication of good knowledge in mathematics, for it is possible to give correct answers to mathematical problems simply by applying the formulæ without understanding a bit of the subject.

The questions in mathematics, therefore, should be so framed and problems so presented as to involve no complex and cumbrous figures. It should be an aim to master the whole science of mathematics, and understand the various mathematical problems and operations by using small and simple figures only, *e.g.*, numbers of three digits. Concrete objects should be placed before the learner to help his power of understanding a problem. A very good method of teaching mathematics is by drawing diagrams and having recourse to geometrical figures. When the mathematical sense has thus been trained and the student has been habituated to solving the varying problems and calculations necessary to human life, it would be time to introduce complexities in the figures and signs and allow the several branches of mathematical science, *e.g.*, Algebra, Geometry, etc., their proper place in the development of his intelligence and knowledge.

SECTION IX

THE STUDY OF NATURAL AND TECHNICAL SCIENCES

WE have thus seen that the inductive method of teaching would require in the case of the human sciences an intimate acquaintance with the various psychical processes and operations, thoughts and ideas, diverse ideals of character and motives of action, multifarious rites and ceremonies, the numberless customs and practices, and the varied institutions and organizations that constitute the several aspects of human and social life. The object underlying this method is to impress upon the reader the vastness, variety, and complexity of the intellectual, social, political, and economic spheres of human activity.

In the case of the physical and natural sciences also the student should be intimately acquainted with the diverse forces of Nature and materials of the physical world in such a way as to realize its vastness and variety. With this object in view, the student of natural sciences would have to follow the incessant changes in the physical universe, and study minutely the different manifestations of Energy and operations of Nature in fire and earth, water and rocks, plants and animals, planets and seasons. The student should thus be familiar with the natural revolutions and transformations going on in this world owing to the influence of these causes, the various forms the world is assuming on account of these, and the thousand and one uses which human beings are making of these forces, materials, and transformations.

By directing his attention to these varieties of natural phenomena the student will have to acquire a knowledge of this physical world. A comprehensive observation of the things around us must by all means be resorted to; the objects in the external world have to be perceived through all the senses. The organs of touch and sight have to be constantly used by the student in thus acquainting himself with the environment, each organ being adapted to its particular object. By this means he will be intimately familiar with the world. This intimate familiarity with it will enable him to understand clearly all its peculiar processes and characteristics, and will, on the one hand, compel Nature to reveal her special features and workings, manifestations and operations, and, on the other, entitle him to question her about her innermost secrets and disclose the most hidden truths.

Thus the student of physics will begin by studying, not the physical energies of nature in the abstract, as is the common practice, but the concrete objects and things of the world. He will take specimens of various classes of objects, *e.g.*, solid, liquid, or gaseous, and study the possible properties of each body. While analysing the properties of the objects the learner will be in a position only to guess the effects of the various energies of nature on each object and get some account of the energies themselves. The natural energies and the laws of their manifestation and operation have to be deduced by the pupil out of the various analyses of physical properties of the objects. They are not to be taken as the data with which to start.

So also in chemistry, instead of studying the elements in the very beginning the student will have to direct his attention to the chemical nature and properties of such material objects as lie around him. A knowledge of the chemical processes in plants, animals, and minerals, *i.e.*, an account of the various ways in which the constituents of the vegetable, mineral, and animal worlds are being transformed, is to be the basis of the study of chemical science. The different chemical properties of each object are to be learnt through multifarious experiments. The student need only analyse or divide the objects and combine or synthetize them and study the varieties in effect. He has to be familiar with the thousand and one analyses and syntheses that constitute the changes in the actual, concrete world in which we live. The chemical elements and the laws of combination will have to be deduced out of these processes and products, and should therefore come at the close of chemical studies.

Just as the student of Physics and Chemistry will have to begin with a study of the various physical and chemical properties of the concrete objects in this world, so the student of geology has to be well grounded at the outset in a knowledge of the diverse changes of nature in land, water, and atmosphere. He has to observe the lithospherical, hydrospherical, and atmospherical facts and phenomena, classify them, and take note of the constant shiftings of their conditions. He will thus have to familiarize himself with the incessant movements and changes of the clouds in shape and size, the motions of the wind, the growth and decay of hills, the windings and shiftings of the course of streams, changes of weather and seasons, etc., and finally use these facts for the detection of the universal principles underlying these changes.

So also the vastness and variety of the vegetable world are to be realized by observing specimens of various kinds of plants. The student of Botany will have to study at the outset not the classification of plants and of their organs, but will have to direct his attention to the individual plants of the locality, and analyse and study their several parts. In studying each plant, the reader has to collect an account of its external and internal characteristics, its growth and development, its habits and habitats, its food and medicines, as well as its utility to human society. Many a plant and shrub, fruit and flower will thus come under his scrutiny. These particular and individual studies of the several specimens will entitle the reader to institute comparisons and bring out points of analogy and contrast between them, and ultimately to classify and generalize them and discover the fundamental principles regulating the life, growth, and developments of the plants. The classification of the plants or the roots and stems should not be the data with the student of botany, but has to be found out by him for himself at the close.

The remarks we have made with regard to the study of plants are equally applicable to the study of animals. The student has to begin with the study and observation of the familiar animals. Their external and internal features, their habits and abodes, the food they eat, and the use that can be made of them by men are the various items of information that are to be collected by the first learners of Zoology.

A knowledge of the external and internal features and peculiarities of plants and lower animals, if and when combined with the same kind of information about human beings, will give the student a knowledge of the various types of living beings inhabiting the world, and supply sufficient data for the formulation of laws governing and controlling the biological sphere. For this purpose the same kind of inquiry that has been suggested with regard to plants and lower animals has to be applied with regard to the physical features and framework of the human beings. With this object in view, the student will have to equip himself at the first instance with a knowledge of the various operations performed by human limbs and muscles, the movements and breathings, circulation of blood and digestion of food, etc.

By thus studying the external manifestations of the life-principle and the varieties of physical actions the pupil will be in a position to master the laws that regulate man's life and health.

We have thus seen that according to the inductive method of teaching the student is placed before the thousand and one facts and phenomena of the mental and physical worlds when he studies literary and scientific subjects. Even so in order to master the agricultural and industrial arts the student has to familiarize himself with the processes of creating the various objects of human use; he must needs observe the various processes of agriculture and manufacture adopted in producing useful commodities. As the natural sciences are learnt by observation and experiment, and the mental sciences are mastered by regard being had to the psychological characteristics of human mind and to the various constituent elements of human society, so also the student has to acquire knowledge in the arts of producing wealth and creating values by resorting to a practical course which involves apprenticeship and study at the farms, workshops, and manufacturing establishments. In subjects like these it is useless to depend upon books and to learn formulæ by rote. The workshop is to be regarded as both the instructor and the training ground.

The prevalent method of imparting knowledge in these subjects requires the students to commit to memory the formulæ in the first instance, and then to undertake certain experiments by way of supplements as illustrative of the formulæ. This is far from what it ought to be. According to the method of teaching on which we have been expatiating so long, books and formulæ are of secondary importance: in it the workshops and laboratories occupy the foremost position. Here the truths arrived at by laboratory experiments are to be endorsed by, and even modify and correct, books if necessary. The theoretical book-knowledge is not to be verified by experiments in the laboratories and workshops. On the other hand, the teachings of the factories and laboratories are to occupy the place, and even to subordinate the use, of books.

SECTION X

GENERAL REMARKS ON THE INDUCTIVE METHOD

A GREAT variety of materials and incidents, thoughts and ideals, actions and deliberations, changes and transformations, processes and appliances has to be placed before the student when the teacher adopts the inductive method of teaching. The student has to examine each object from various standpoints, and various aspects of each subject have to be studied. When a sufficient number of facts has been accumulated, and each subject minutely examined and analysed, materials will be ready for the formulation of theories and hypotheses regarding their common nature and characteristics and the laws of their working. When these hypotheses and guess-works about the causal relations and order of occurrences have been well tested and brought into relation with one another, the path will be opened up for the discovery and formulation of the unity in the diversity, and the "scientific" truth about the subject. Finally, there will have sprung up a body of truths systematized and organized—in other words, a science.

In the foregoing pages we have only made very brief remarks of a general nature on the inductive method. We have not said how this method will have to be modified with the progress of the pupil in each of the subjects that falls within the range of study. We have also omitted to mention the defects and imperfections of this system. It is in contemplation to bring out a work which will deal with these points elaborately.

SECTION XI

FOREWORD TO THE BOOK

THE plan of this book will be as follows:

Vol. I divides itself into a number of parts, according to the educational ideals among the different nations of the world, such as the Hindus, the Greeks, and the Egyptians, etc.

Vol. II will be subdivided into two parts. The first will treat of the theory and philosophy of education and the general principles regarding its nature, aims, and means; the second will be devoted to sketching out the best system of education that is adapted to the requirements of the Indians of the modern age.

Vol. III is the practical portion of the whole work. This resolves itself into as many parts as there are subjects for study, *e.g.*, Language, Literature, Chemistry, Mathematics, Zoology, etc.

Enormous labour and patience as well as a good deal of time are necessary to complete a work like this. Want of time, owing to multiplicity of duties and inadequate knowledge in many branches, are likely to be hindrances. Besides, the comprehensive method set forth in these pages is being put into practice ; for methods of teaching cannot be established if we have no opportunity of testing them, and their defects cannot be detected unless the application is watched while instructing students of various ages and capacities. For these reasons a number of scholars are being trained up who will adopt this method of teaching in their tutorial work.

SECTION XII

PLEA FOR THE WORK

IN conclusion I take this opportunity of frankly confessing that it may have been a sort of presumption on my part to attempt such a work as requires encyclopædic knowledge and a varied experience. But it is not the glory of having accomplished an almost impossible task that has actuated me to undertake it. Incompetent as I am, I make this attempt, however humble, to supply one of the crying wants of our country. I sincerely hope and believe that men of real ability will soon come forward to apply their energy in this direction and maintain the dignity of the undertaking.

I find unmistakable indications in our society and can understand from the signs of the times that in no distant future the question of education will assume momentous importance and engross the attention of our scholars and public men. Our workers and thinkers and educated men in general will more and more take upon themselves the responsibility of conducting the educational movement, and will volunteer to be pillars of various educational institutions. Mass education and female education, technical and commercial education, methods of teaching and education in research work, the training of teachers, and other problems connected with the great question of national education will occupy the foremost place in the people's thought. According to the new moral sense and novel standard of moral judgment that are gradually becoming parts of our national consciousness, the highest form of patriotism and philanthropy will be displayed by him who devotes his whole life to the diffusion of learning and spread of education among the people. And these activities will control and govern all other movements in the country. The educational enthusiasm of the nation will grow wider and deeper, and ultimately swallow up all other propagandisms. Workers and organizers in the interest of India's regeneration will consider their sole religion to be the foundation of such temples of learning as help forward the development of manhood of her teeming millions, and choose to appreciate their highest self-realization in applying themselves whole-heartedly and devoting their whole time and energy to the furtherance of this object. Idealists and self-sacrificing men will sincerely and earnestly flock to the field of education. The diffusion of man-making culture is, in fact, soon going to be an all-absorbing aim, the life's mission of some of our best men, and to be exalted into a new form of Sanyâsa and penance in our social system. From among educators will come the Sanyâsis and missionaries of Young India.